Hands-On Essays

Bonita Lillie Publishing
Charlotte, North Carolina

Many thanks to my family and talented friends who helped produce this curriculum. I couldn't have done it without you!

Hands-On Essays
Copyright © 2008, 2010, 2013 by Bonita Lillie
Cover design by Charis Pope
Images by Angie Sinclair from Clipart.com

Published by:
Bonita Lillie Publishing
Charlotte, North Carolina
www.handsonessays.com

"Humpty Dumpty" rhyme quoted with permission by Marjorie Ainsborough Decker, copyright owner and author of the Christian Mother Goose *Rock-A-Bye Bible.* Copyright 1987 Marjorie Decker.

Reproduction of this work in any form or language, or by any means, electronic or mechanical, including photocopying, recording, or by any retrieval system, is prohibited without express written permission from the publisher.

03-15-13

DEDICATION

I dedicate this curriculum to every student
who has ever taken my writing classes.
You make my heart sing!

I also dedicate it to my dear friend, Tina Gilbert,
who was the first to ask, "Will you teach my kids to write?"

An Important Note from the Author

Hi Friends,

I'm so glad you've chosen to use *Hands-On Essays* to improve your writing skills. In order to get the most out of the curriculum, I invite you to visit the *Hands-On Essays* website at www.handsonessays.com .

The website is where you will find instructional videos to accompany each lesson in the curriculum. You can also visit the website to sign up for my newsletter which offers tips for writers of all ages, additional help with writing essays, and updates on the latest publications from Bonita Lillie Publishing. If you have questions, feel free to email me via the contact form on the website.

Have fun mastering the essay!

Blessings,
Bonita Lillie

Table of Contents

Student Section

How to Use This Curriculum 2
Lesson 1: Hands-On Essays Demonstration 3-5
Lesson 2: Know Your Audience 6-7
Lesson 3: Choosing a Topic 8-10
Lesson 4: Outlining the Essay 11-14
Lesson 5: Hooking the Reader 15-20
Lesson 6: Creating a Thesis Statement 21-23
Lesson 7: Developing the Body of the Essay 24-27
Lesson 8: Writing the Conclusion 28-30
Lesson 9: Descriptive Essays 31-36
Lesson 10: Comparing/Contrasting Essays 37-42
Lesson 11: Persuasive Essays 43-48
Lesson 12: Revising the Essay 49-52
Lesson 13: Developing Your Writing Style 53-60
Lesson 14: Understanding Prompts 61-64
Lesson 15: Timed Writing 65-67
Lesson 16: The Wrap Up 68-69
Writing Ideas 70-74

Resources for Research Topics 75
Proofreading Checklist 88

Parent/Evaluator Section

How to Evaluate Writing 76
Lesson by Lesson Evaluations 77-84
Suggested Essay Assignments 85-87

How to Use This Curriculum

Let me guess. You're not too excited about writing essays. Maybe you think writing is boring or difficult. Writing *can* be both boring and difficult, but it doesn't have to be that way. Writing can be fun. It's all in the way you approach it.

When was the last time writing made you laugh? When was the last time you went wild with creativity? Have you ever really written what *you* think or feel? What if you had a curriculum that allowed you to write and still be you? Welcome to *Hands-On Essays*!

In this course you will learn a step-by-step method for writing essays. Each lesson is so simple. This is what you'll do:

1. Watch the video lesson at www.handsonessays.com .
2. Read the key points for the lesson.
3. Look at the writing samples.
4. Do the hands-on writing activities listed.

It's that easy! No fuss, no complicated curriculum to wade through, it's all very direct and simple. Move at your own pace and take as much time as you need to learn the material in each lesson. To start, choose a special notebook to hold the papers you'll write. Decorate it in your own unique style. Then relax and enjoy *Hands-On Essays*. When you finish you'll feel much more confident about writing essays. YOU CAN DO IT!

> *The worst thing you write is better than the best thing you didn't write.* -unknown

Lesson 1: Hands-On Essay Demonstration

Goal: Learn the essay format.

 Watch the video lesson titled, *Hands-On Essay Demonstration*, and become familiar with the standard essay format.

Key Points:

 An essay is an organized piece of writing that centers on one theme or topic.

 A standard essay is generally five paragraphs in length.

 Your thumb represents the first paragraph, the introduction.

The introduction, or first paragraph, introduces the topic and contains the hook and thesis statement.

Your three middle fingers represent the three middle paragraphs of the essay, also called the body. These paragraphs contain the bulk of the writing and information in the essay.

Your pinky finger represents the final paragraph, or conclusion, of the essay. It wraps it up and brings it to a close.

A closed fist stands for a well written essay which delivers an impact to the reader.

The pen is the tongue of the mind.
-Miguel de Cervantes

Writing Sample

Now that you know the essay format, it's time to actually read one. In the following essay, Dana tells us about her favorite place.

My Heart is at Home

How would you like to go to a place where everyone thinks you're special? When you wake up in the morning you're surrounded by all the things you love. To top it off, there is no other place that makes you feel as comfortable. Well, that's what makes my home my favorite place!

Love lives in my home. We may not always get along, but we really love each other. Even when I do something wrong I always feel forgiven. If I ever feel lost or alone, I know that at home I am not.

All the things I love and do are available right in my house. My favorite thing to do is listen to music while I draw something from my imagination. At home, I also have sports equipment, my skateboard, my skates, and my bike. My friends can come over and hang out. I can end the day watching T.V. in my pajamas and eating popcorn.

Home is like my favorite pillow. Every way I turn I'm comfortable. I feel at ease whether I'm alone or surrounded by my family. When I'm in a situation that makes me feel like I'm in "Kansas", I click my heels and remind myself, "There's no place like home."

Sure amusement parks are fun and wild. Tropical islands even call my name. But when it comes to a long term relationship no place compares to home.

Dana M. – age 12

Hands-On Activities

 Watch the video lesson again and practice naming the parts of a standard essay using your own hand.

 Trace your hand on a separate paper. Label the parts of an essay.

 Use your own hand to demonstrate the parts of an essay to someone else.

 Continue practicing the essay format until you know it like the back of your hand. Wherever you go in life you will always be able to look at your hand and remember the pattern for a standard essay.

 Do not move on to the next lesson until you are certain you know the essay format without watching the video or looking at the book.

Lesson 2: Know Your Audience

> Goal: Identify your audience and understand their expectations.

 Watch the video lesson titled, *Know Your Audience.*

Key Points

☞ Why do you need to know your audience? You can't write for the whole world. In order to meet the expectations of your particular audience, knowing whom you're writing for will help you determine what information, details, and tone to use in your essay.

☞ Ask yourself, "Who is my audience and what do they expect from me?"

☞ Decide what you want your audience to take away from your paper.

☞ Many essays that you write will be for academic audiences, which may include teachers, parents, fellow students, college professors, or SAT evaluators.

☞ An academic audience will expect your essay to:
- be well written and grammatically correct
- follow the essay format
- show that the writer is knowledgeable about the subject
- contain facts or concrete examples
- have a degree of professionalism

Over the next several lessons you will write an expository essay. An expository essay explains, informs, instructs, or clarifies.

It took me fifteen years to discover I had no talent for writing, but I couldn't give it up because by that time I was too famous.
-Robert Benchley

Hands-On Activities

 Watch the video lesson again. Pay close attention to the nursery rhyme that I read at the beginning of the lesson. Discuss the following questions with your class or teacher, or answer them in writing.
 1. Who is the appropriate audience for a nursery rhyme?
 2. What would this particular audience expect from a writer?

 Think about each of the following audiences and what each group would expect from a writer. Write down your ideas, or discuss them with your class or teacher.
- a politician
- an English teacher
- a group of your friends
- a group of corporate business people

 In the next lesson you will begin writing an expository essay. Be thinking about the following questions.
 1. Who is my audience? Choose or determine who your audience will be.
 2. What will they expect from me?

Lesson 3: Choosing a Topic

Goal: Choose and develop a topic for an essay.

 Watch the video lesson titled, *Choosing a Topic.*

Key Points

 The first step to writing an essay is choosing an appropriate topic.

 To help choose a topic, ask yourself the following questions.
- What do I like?
- What do I know?
- What makes me happy?
- What makes me sad?
- What makes me angry?
- What do I seek to understand?
- What do I want to change?

 It's easiest to write about things that you like and know.

 Once you decide on a topic, you will need to brainstorm. You can do this by creating an idea web (see page 9).

 If you have to write on a topic you know little about, you will need to do some research to determine what information to share with your reader. Page 75 lists resources that may be helpful.

Write what you like; there is no other rule.
-O. Henry

Writing Sample

 My topic is Black Widow spiders and this is my idea web.

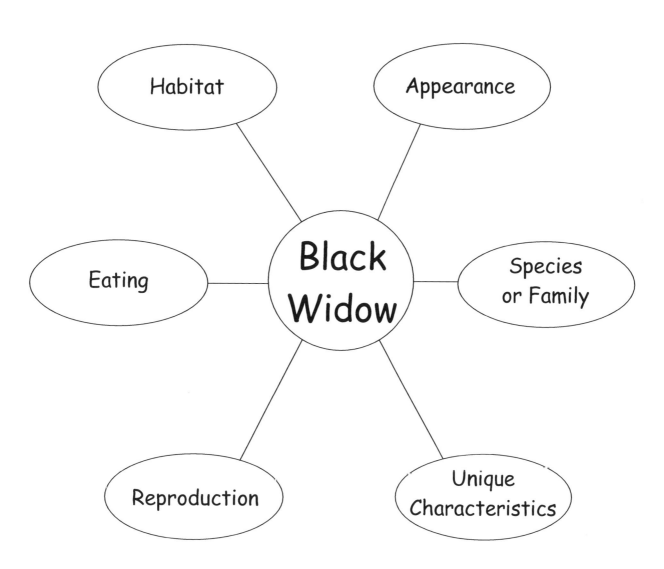

Hands-On Activities

 Write down your answers, or discuss them with your class or your teacher:
- What do I like?
- What do I know?
- What makes me happy?
- What makes me sad?
- What makes me angry?
- What do I seek to understand?
- What do I want to change?

 Use your answers to the questions above to choose a topic for your expository essay. Some topics for expository essays are also listed on page 70.

 Brainstorm your topic. You can do this by creating an idea web on paper, or you can use simple objects to actually create a web similar to the one seen on the video. For example, you might use toothpicks, string, and index cards to make a physical idea web, or you can draw your idea web on a marker board.

Lesson 4: Outlining the Essay

Goal: Write an outline for your essay.

 Watch the video lesson titled, *Outlining the Essay*.

Key Points

 An outline is like a skeleton. It provides structure, support, organization, and a logical flow.

 The outline is for the writer, not the reader. It helps organize the writer's thoughts.

 Since the reader won't see the outline, it doesn't need to be written in complete sentences.

 The *Hands-On Essays* format provides a skeleton, or outline, for an essay. All you need to do is fill in the details of the various parts.

 Your thumb represents the introduction, or first paragraph, of an essay.

 The first paragraph of the essay introduces the topic, includes a hook which grabs the reader's attention, and ends with a thesis statement.

 The introduction is the most important paragraph in the essay because:
- It makes the first impression on the reader.
- It introduces the topic and tells the reader what to expect in the essay.
- It sets the tone of the essay (humorous, formal, etc.).

The introduction is usually shaped like a funnel. It starts wide and general, and gets more narrow and specific. The last sentence of the introduction is the thesis statement, which explains the topic of the essay.

> *Writing is long periods of thinking and short periods of writing.*
> *-Ernest Hemingway*

Writing Sample

This is the outline for my essay about Black Widow spiders:

Title: The Widow's Website

Introduction (first paragraph):
    Hook: a scary scene
    Thesis statement: It's a fascinating creature because of its appearance, web, and unique characteristics.

Body:
    Second paragraph- unusual appearance
        Supporting evidence:
- long legs
- ball shaped black body
- 1.5 inches in diameter
- red hourglass on underside

    Third paragraph- web for shelter and food
        Supporting evidence:
- dark areas
- no shape or form
- stronger silk than other spiders
- hangs belly upward
- sucks liquid from insects
- cuts carcasses free

    Fourth paragraph- unique characteristics
        Supporting evidence:
- cannibal- eats mate and offspring
- more poisonous than a rattlesnake
- symptoms to humans

Conclusion (fifth paragraph):
- Restate thesis in a new way.
- She's black, but not in mourning.

Hands-On Activities

 Review the idea web from your brainstorming session. Decide what information to use in your essay. Decide what topics can be combined and what can be left out.

 Follow the *Hands-On Essays* pattern and the sample on page 13 to begin the creation of the outline for your expository essay. You will continue working on the outline as you work your way through the next few lessons.

Lesson 5: Hooking the Reader

> Goal: Write an opening statement that will grab the reader's attention.

 Watch the video lesson titled, *Hooking the Reader.*

Key Points

 The thumb represents the hook. Thumbs up!

 The hook grabs the reader's attention and makes him want to continue reading the essay. It's like the bait on a fishhook. The fish bites it, and the fisherman reels him in.

 Avoid these types of beginnings:
- This paper is about...
- In this essay, I'm going to write about...
- Jumping in and giving information about the topic without an introduction.
    - Example of a poor introduction:
    Black Widow spiders are arachnids.
- Overused expressions such as:
    It was a dark and stormy night.

 A title can be a hook:
- Unusual title: *My Neighbors Are Old Goats*
- Alliteration: *Fussin', Fightin,' and Forgivin'*
- Rearrange a familiar title, quote, or name of a book, movie, or song: *War and Peas*

☞ Types of hooks:

1. Question- causes the reader to participate because a question needs an answer

2. Interesting facts- arouses the reader's curiosity

3. Setting the scene- gets the reader's imagination involved

4. Dialogue- draws the reader into the relationship

5. Powerful description- engages the reader's senses

6. Action- gives a sense of adventure

7. Element of surprise- takes the reader off-guard

8. Powerful quote- the reader identifies with the person quoted

9. Brief story- everybody loves a story

10. Appropriate humor- makes the reader laugh

What is written without effort is generally read without pleasure.
-Samuel Johnson

Writing Sample

Question:

Are you tired of getting out of your nice warm bed and putting on freezing clothes?
Chad G. - age 15

How would you like it if someone came into your peaceful turkey farm and took you away from all twenty-three brothers, nineteen sisters, and your poor mother?
Bobby Z. - age 15

If you found a doorway to another world, would you want to open it or would you seal it permanently? Would you try to harness its power or would you try and destroy it? What if you couldn't destroy it? What if you couldn't open it? Or worse, what if it was open and you couldn't seal it? What if it pulled you in too fast to even make that decision?
Jeremy W. – age 13

Interesting Facts:

I figured out why they call this place the ice planet. It's -373 degrees Fahrenheit here!
Breanne L. – age 11

The Acura NSX has a supercharged Doch Vtec V6 engine with the power of 290 horses along with 224 human foot pounds of torque.
David L.- age 13

Setting the Scene:

Imagine a large room in a research center at Duke University. As I walk into the room I see several doctors in lab coats. Some are wearing stethoscopes, others have gloves on their hands, and the rest are holding clipboards as they walk by. When I enter the room I smell different types of chemicals and fumes of smoke from Bunsen burners that have soured the air. Test tubes and flasks act like prisms separating the sunlight coming through the windows. Cages full of cedar chips house lab rats, hamsters, and mice. Dissecting kits for amphibians are open and ready for use. Each lab cubicle has a microscope, chair, pencil, and paper.
Jackie M.- age 13

Dialogue:

"Let's celebrate!" one of the mathematicians said triumphantly after several U.S. mathematicians discovered the largest known prime number.
Rachel I.- age 13

"And sixteen cents is your change. Thank you and come again." Mr. Robert Hiss said thank you and walked to his car.
Bobby Z. - age 15

Powerful Description:

I was roaming through the cold ocean that day. My stomach was empty and I could feel it growling. I hadn't eaten in ten minutes and I was starving for food.
Allison W. – age 13

Sweat raced down my face and back. My heart beat wildly. My legs throbbed with pain and I felt as though every cell in my body would burst at any moment. Marriage proposals aren't easy!
B.L.

Action:

Ring…ring…ring…John Matheson's cell phone rang. He politely excused himself from the restaurant table where he was having a business lunch with a client.
Jared D. – age 13

Emily ran down the stairs to answer the door. Grandma Miller was coming to visit and she was finally here!
Allison W. – age 13

Element of Surprise:

After packaging up pork tenderloin and ribeye steaks, Genghis Porterhouse Korfin, owner of Ghengis Meats, was sharpening his knives when a large monster smashed through his window.
Rachel I.- age 13

Seven o'clock and all is silent. Eight o'clock and all is silent. Ten o'clock and all is silent. And then here it comes- the smell of pizza through my bedroom door.
Jared D. – age 13

Brief Story:

For one brief day I was a celebrity. It happened when I was a mere three years old. A reporter spied me eating cotton candy during a parade. He bought another round and started snapping pictures. The next day my bouncy brown curls and cotton candy beard appeared on the front page of the Mt. Holly newspaper. Of course, no one knew about it because my grandpa bought every paper around.
B.L.

Powerful Quote:

I have a dream! (Martin Luther King, Jr.)
B.L.

Early to bed, early to rise, makes a man healthy, wealthy and wise, but it might also make him grumpy!
B.L.

Humor

(To the tune of All I Want for Christmas is My Two Front Teeth)
All I want for Christmas is some dirt bike boots,
Some dirt bike boots,
Oh, some dirt bike boots.
Gee, if I could only have some dirt bike boots,
Then I would have a Merry Christmas.
Chad G.- age 15

About 5823 days, 8 hours, and 43 minutes ago a little pink blob of skin was born. He was a handsome blob and his name was Austin.
Austin W.- age 16

Read the hook from my expository essay about Black Widow spiders.

In the murky shadows she silently waits, a merciless killer hidden by the cover of darkness. One tiny insect, a slight web vibration, and she darts in for the kill.

Hands-On Activities

 Read through the sample hooks. Choose a few types that you think would work best for your expository essay.

 Write some sample hooks. Read them to a few people and watch for their reactions.

 Choose the hook you think best fits your expository essay, and add it to your outline from Lesson 4.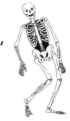

Lesson 6: Creating a Thesis Statement

> Goal: Create a thesis statement that clearly states the topic of the essay.

 Watch the video lesson titled,
Creating a Thesis Statement.

Key Points

👉 The thesis statement is the sentence that states the subject of the essay. It's like a map that shows the reader where the essay is going.

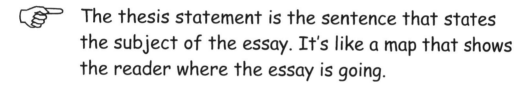

👉 Sometimes it's a good idea to write the thesis statement first, prior to outlining or writing the other parts of the paper, so that you will have a clear picture of what you're going to say in the essay.

👉 Ask yourself, "What do I want to say?" If you don't know, no one else will know either.

👉 The thesis statement must be clear.
- It's usually best to write one clear sentence.
- Use simple language.
- If you can't write a thesis statement, you don't have a clear picture of your topic.

The thesis statement must be focused.
- Stick to one topic.
- The thesis statement can be used as a mini outline for the body of the essay. For example, let's pretend I'm writing an essay about the benefits of teenagers having jobs, and this is my thesis statement: *Working a job will teach a teenager responsibility, time management, and how to budget money.*
- The reader can expect me to talk about responsibility first, time management second, and budgeting money third.

 The thesis statement must be present in the first paragraph of the essay, and restated in a new way in the last paragraph.

> *You can't sit around and wait for inspiration.*
> *You have to go after it with a club.*
> *-Jack London*

Writing Sample

Simple Thesis Statements:

Dirt bike boots are the key to being safe on a dirt bike. Chad G.- age 15

I believe black holes exist. George S. - age 14

Thesis statements that outline the body of the essay:

The best European countries to visit are England, Italy, and France. B.L.

Cats make great pets because they are affectionate, easy to care for, and quick learners. B. L.

This is the introduction for my expository essay.
The thesis statement is found at the end of the paragraph.

In the murky shadows she silently waits, a merciless killer hidden by the cover of darkness. One tiny insect, a slight web vibration, and she darts in for the kill. This is the world of the infamous arachnid known as the Black Widow. The Black Widow is a fascinating creature that has an unusual appearance, uses a web for shelter and catching prey, and has several unique characteristics that set it apart from other spiders.

Hands-On Activities

 Write a single-sentence thesis statement for your expository essay.

 Write your thesis statement on a slip of paper. Ask someone to read it, but don't reveal the subject of your essay. After the person reads the thesis statement, ask him to tell you the main topic of your essay. If the other person can't clearly see the topic of your essay from your thesis statement alone, you probably need to rewrite it in a more direct, clear way.

 Choose the thesis statement you think best fits your expository essay, and add it to your outline begun in Lesson 4.

 Now that you've written both a hook and a thesis statement, it's time to go ahead and write the first paragraph, or introduction, of your expository essay.

Lesson 7: Developing the Body of the Essay

Goal: Write the three middle paragraphs of the essay.

 Watch the video lesson titled,
Developing the Body of the Essay.

Key Points

 Your three middle fingers represent the body of the essay.

 Each paragraph should have a clear topic sentence. A topic sentence is a sentence that tells the main subject of the paragraph, and is usually the first sentence of the paragraph. For example, if you want to write a paragraph about your best friend's humor, the topic sentence might be: *My best friend is really funny.*

 Each topic sentence should be a point that further explains the thesis statement. For example, if the thesis statement is, "The best European countries to visit are England, Italy, and France," then the topic sentence for the first paragraph of the body could be, "Touring England's castles is educational and fun."

 The body of the essay contains the bulk of the writing, the details, and the evidence to support the topic sentence of each paragraph.

 I've listed some ways you can provide details and evidence.
- Use personal examples from your own life or the lives of others.
- Include a brief story that illustrates your point.
- Use a quote or excerpt from a book or other publication.
- Give an example based on something you've studied in school.
- Use statistics.

Writing Sample

The following examples show how to provide evidence for the points you want to make in the body of your essay.

Personal Example:

Topic Sentence: Softball is a dangerous sport.

Evidence: In the past few years, three of my teammates broke bones. One broke her ankle, another broke her tail bone, and yet another broke her arm. I got hit in the forehead and sprained my ankle.
Breanne L.- age 12

Brief Story:

Topic Sentence: Boxers are smart dogs.

Evidence: Our neighbor had a Boxer that was a friend to our dog. She figured out that she could escape her electric fence if she was willing to endure a moment of pain. She came to our yard on multiple occasions, unlatched our gate, and let herself in the back yard. She even taught our dog how to let himself out of the back yard.
B.L.

Quote or Excerpt from a Publication:

Topic Sentence: A government should not only enforce the laws, but also protect its people from those who would do harm.

Evidence: A famous man once said, "The price of freedom is eternal vigilance."
Johnnie C.- age 14

Example Based on Something You've Studied:

Topic Sentence: Smoking cigarettes can do many harmful things to your health.

Evidence: Nicotine causes clots that prevent oxygen from going to the entire body and it extracts oxygen from cells as it moves through your system.
George S.- age 14

Example using Statistics:

Topic Sentence: Overall, you can see that smoking is not a good idea.

Evidence: It is the number one cause of deaths in the United States, killing over 400,000 people each year.
George S.- age 14

Writing Sample

Read the three middle paragraphs, or body, of my expository essay. Each topic sentence is underlined.

<u>I think the Black Widow has an elegant, almost ladylike appearance. Long slender legs support her shiny ball shaped body.</u> With her legs spread out she's roughly 1.5 inches in diameter. She uses those legs to make swift, graceful movements. You might say she has an hourglass figure, at least on her underside where she sports a red hourglass marking. Indeed, she's the fashion model of the spider family.

<u>For all of her good looks, the Black Widow is not a socialite, but is quite shy and makes her residence in dark, secluded areas.</u> She's not much of a housekeeper as her web has no particular shape or form. However, she uses only the finest, strongest silk to weave it. Most of the time you can find her hanging around the house, belly upward, awaiting the arrival of dinner. When an unlucky insect wanders into her web, supper is served. This is when things get gross. She punctures the insect's hard shell and sucks out all the liquid contents within it. After the meal she tidies up by cutting the carcasses free from her web.

<u>It's her unique habits that I find most fascinating.</u> She's a cannibal. She mates only once in her lifetime and usually makes a meal of her mate. She lays egg sacs with 250-700 eggs each, but her offspring better scurry or they'll be a midnight snack. Only about 1-2 per sac will live to adulthood. Yet, her most vicious trait is her potent neurotoxic venom which is fifteen times as toxic as a prairie rattlesnake. She doesn't usually inject enough to kill a human, but the poison can cause some nasty side effects like aching, profuse sweating, headaches, increased blood pressure, nausea, and breathing difficulties. As you can see, she's not the friendly sort.

> *I love being a writer. What I can't stand is the paperwork.* — Peter De Vries

Hands-On Activities

 Watch the video lesson again. This time record the evidence found in each room of the house which proved that Goldilocks had been there.

Living room   1. _____

2. _____

3. _____

Kitchen   1. _____

2. _____

3. _____

Bedrooms   1. _____

2. _____

3. _____

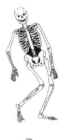

 Now that you've written a basic outline for the three middle paragraphs of the Goldilocks story, it is time to select the topics and supporting evidence for the three middle paragraphs of your essay. Record this information in your outline begun in Lesson 4.

 Write the three middle paragraphs of your expository essay.

Lesson 8: Writing the Conclusion

Goal: Write a concluding paragraph that wraps up the essay.

 Watch the video lesson titled, *Writing the Conclusion..*

Key Points

  The pinky finger represents the conclusion.

  The conclusion may summarize the essay by rewording the thesis statement in a new way.

  No new information or evidence should be included in the conclusion.

  The conclusion leaves the reader with something to think about, similar to the hook in the first paragraph.

How vain it is to sit down to write when you have not stood up to live.
- Henry David Thoreau

Writing Sample

Read my entire essay about Black Widows. Pay special attention to the conclusion at the end.

The Widow's Website

   In the murky shadows she silently waits, a merciless killer hidden by the cover of darkness. One tiny insect, a slight web vibration, and she darts in for the kill. This is the world of the infamous arachnid known as the Black Widow. <u>The Black Widow is a fascinating creature that has an unusual appearance, uses a web for shelter and catching prey, and has several unique characteristics that set it apart from other spiders.</u>

   I think the Black Widow has an elegant, almost ladylike appearance. Long slender legs support her shiny ball shaped body. With her legs spread out she's roughly 1.5 inches in diameter. She uses those legs to make swift, graceful movements. You might say she has an hourglass figure, at least on her underside where she sports a red hourglass marking. Indeed, she's the fashion model of the spider family.

   For all of her good looks, the Black Widow is not a socialite, but is quite shy and makes her residence in dark, secluded areas. She's not much of a housekeeper as her web has no particular shape or form. However, she uses only the finest, strongest silk to weave it. Most of the time you can find her hanging around the house, belly upward, awaiting the arrival of dinner. When an unlucky insect wanders into her web, supper is served. This is when things get gross. She punctures the insect's hard shell and sucks out all the liquid contents within it. After the meal she tidies up by cutting the carcasses free from her web.

   It's her unique habits that I find most fascinating. She's a cannibal. She mates only once in her lifetime and usually makes a meal of her mate. She lays egg sacs with 250-700 eggs each, but her offspring better scurry or they'll be a midnight snack. Only about 1-2 per sac will live to adulthood. Yet, her most vicious trait is her potent neurotoxic venom which is fifteen times as toxic as a prairie rattlesnake. She doesn't usually inject enough to kill a human, but the poison can cause some nasty side effects like aching, profuse sweating, headaches, increased blood pressure, nausea, and breathing difficulties. As you can see, she's not the friendly sort.

With her regal appearance, cob-like web, and unfriendly gestures, the Black Widow has a wicked reputation, but I think she's a wondrous creation of God. One thing is for sure. This husbandless spider may be dressed in black, but she's certainly not in mourning.

Hands-On Activities

 Decide how to summarize your conclusion, and add this information to your outline begun in Lesson 4.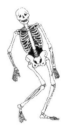

 Write the conclusion for your expository essay.

Put all the pieces of your expository essay together, and type it or write it in your best handwriting.

 CONGRATULATIONS! You've completed your first essay. Give yourself a round of applause.

Lesson 9: Descriptive Essays

Goal: Write a descriptive essay.

 Watch the video lesson titled, *Descriptive Essays.*

Key Points

 A descriptive essay describes something so that the reader can sense it.

 Show your reader, don't just tell. This means that you paint a picture with your words.

 In order to describe something well, a writer must observe it with as many of the five senses as possible: sight, smell, hearing, touch, and taste.

Example: *I'm standing on the beach looking at an endless ocean that stretches to the horizon (sight). Squishy sand envelops my feet as cool water splashes my toes (touch). A faint, warm breeze carries the scent of suntan oil (smell), and I can almost taste the saltiness in the air (taste). The high-pitched screech of hovering seagulls grabs my attention (hearing). The place where shore and water meet is like no other place on earth.*

☞ An adjective is a word that describes a noun.

- *tie-dyed* shirt
- *dry, frizzy* hair
- *tasteless, waterlogged* pasta

☞ A simile compares two things using the words *like* or *as*.
- Junior drives *like* a bull in a china shop.
- Dad's gym bag is *as* stinky *as* a room full of teenage boys who forgot to use deodorant.

☞ A metaphor compares two things without using the words *like* or *as*.
- On cleaning day Mom is a tornado.
- Grandma is a lightning bolt behind the wheel of her new sports car.

I saw the angel in the marble and carved until I set it free. -Michelangelo

Writing Sample

Read the following descriptive essay where Camryn tells about a favorite family member.

Noel

One member of my family is different from all the rest. She is quite hairy. Her name is Noel, and she is my dog. To tell you all about Noel would probably take fiver pages, so I'll only tell you a little bit about her.

First of all, she is black with white markings on her paws and snout that look like polka-dots. She also has big brown eyes that are absolutely adorable. Noel is very hyper, like a child that just had a lot of candy. She is also a hunting dog, so when she is sniffing around and spots something her tail sticks straight out like an arrow and one of her front paws comes up.

Noel is a smart dog. She loves human food, but her favorite is peanut butter. She knows to stop, drop, and roll in case of a fire, also known as sit, lay down, and roll over. Noel knows more tricks such as "shake" and she can pick which hand holds a treat. Noel, as silly as she is, will chase her tail like a merry-go-round in the park. She also loves to play catch and tug-of-war.

Noel is a very sneaky dog too. When I've been lying on my bed and I get up, Noel will take my spot because it's warm. She will do the same thing on the couch. Bath is one of the worst words to say around Noel. She hates baths like a cat hates water. When she hears anyone talking about her bath she runs and hides under the table. To get your attention, Noel will also bark continuously while you're trying to concentrate on school.

Even though Noel can be annoying, mean, and destructive, she can be a very good dog at times. I'm glad I got Noel. She is my dog.

Camryn H.- age 13

Hands-On Activities

 Watch the video lesson again. This time select a piece of food and use it to do the observation exercise along with the DVD lesson.   List your describing words here:

 SIGHT-

 SMELL-

 HEARING-

 TOUCH-

 TASTE-

 Complete the worksheet called, *That Amazing World of Awesome Accurate Adjectives*, on page 35.

 Read through Camryn's essay on page 33. Specifically look for similes and underline them.

 On page 36, practice painting pictures with your words by changing telling statements to showing statements.

 Use the steps for writing an essay to write a descriptive essay about a person, place, or thing. Some topics for descriptive essays are listed on page 71.

When choosing adjectives, it's important not to choose words that are *good* or *bad*. You also don't want to make a *wonderful, outstanding* choice that is totally *fantastic,* but tells little about the word being modified. In fact, when deciding among adjectives, only one will do--the accurate one! Change the adjectives in the sentences below into words that will paint a clear picture in the mind of the reader.

Example: Ben is a good carpenter.
Revision: Ben is an expert carpenter.

1. Ginger is a good singer.

2. Paris is an amazing place!

3. He had a bad day.

4. I just read an awesome story.

5. The weather is pretty today.

6. My friend drives a nice car.

Show, Don't Tell!

Read the following example that converts telling to showing.

Telling: Joe was bored in class.

Showing: Joe stared at the clock, but the time never seemed to change. When would class be over? The teacher's monotonous voiced droned on as Joe glanced out the window. The sky was a colorless gray, a few motionless cars sat in the parking lot, and not a soul was stirring. His attention turned to the bushy-haired girl in front of him. He made an arsenal of spitwads, and one by one flicked them into her hair. When he was satisfied that she looked like she had a bad case of dandruff, he started mindlessly doodling on the edges of his paper. He glanced at the clock. Only ten minutes had passed. When would class be over?

It's your turn. On a separate piece of paper, change these telling statements to showing.

1. The bathroom at the gas station is dirty.
2. Oscar is a funny guy.
3. The weather is bad.

Lesson 10: Comparing/Contrasting Essays

> Goal: Write a comparing/contrasting essay.

 Watch the video lesson titled,
Comparing/Contrasting Essays.

Key Points

☞ Compare to show the similarities between two or more things

☞ Contrast to show the differences between two or more things

☞ A Venn diagram is a tool that can be used to compare and contrast things. An example is on page 38.

☞ In a comparing/contrasting essay, write about your weakest ideas first. For example, if you want to emphasize the similarities, mention the differences first. Leave the reader thinking about the strongest idea at the end.

☞ Point out the reason you're comparing or contrasting the two things. Example: *Living in the city and living in the country both provide educational opportunities.*

☞ You can organize the three middle paragraphs of a comparing/contrasting essay in any of the following ways:

- compare/contrast   - comparing   - contrasting
- compare/contrast   - comparing   - contrasting
- compare/contrast   - contrasting   - comparing

> *I hear and I forget; I see and I remember; I write and I understand.*   *- Chinese Proverb*

Writing Sample

Prior to writing the essay on the following page, Breanne created the Venn diagram below that shows the similarities between her and Elise. Their similarities are recorded in the middle part where the circles intersect, and their differences are written in the outer portions of the circles. A Venn diagram is used to brainstorm ideas, but not every idea has to be used in your essay.

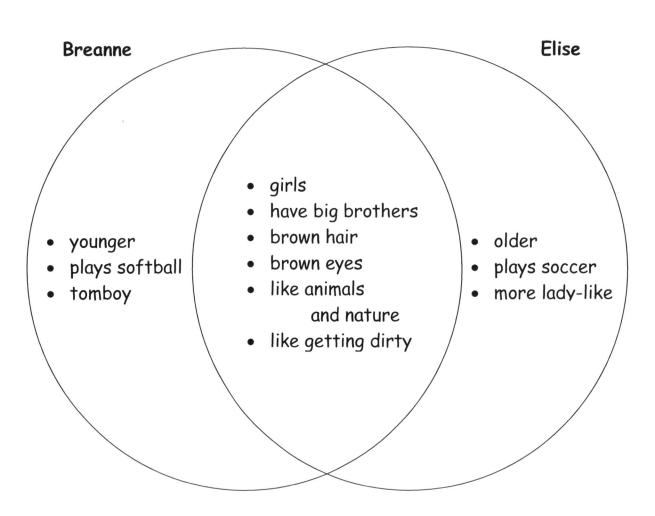

Writing Sample

This essay compares and contrasts Elise and Breanne using this pattern: compare/contrast
                           compare/contrast
                           compare/contrast

My Best Friend and Me

    My best friend, Elise, and I are very alike, but we are also very different. We are like two peas in a pod most of the time, but every now and then we realize how different we really are.

    Both Elise and I like animals, nature, and being outside when it's warm. I prefer watching smaller animals and seeing what they do, but Elise likes taking care of animals such as horses or any animals that she can take home and nurse back to health.

    Elise and I have always been rather tomboyish. We still are, but in different ways. I like softball and Elise likes soccer. One thing we both agree on is that nothing is better than getting good and dirty sometimes.
When it comes to acting ladylike, we're still working on it. I would have to say Elise is better at it than I am because she's older.

    The two of us enjoy volunteer work and we both love working with little children, but we have very different ideas as to what our futures hold. Elise has always known that she would work in the fashion industry, designing jewelry or clothes. I, on the other hand, am not sure what I want to do when I grow up. I know I want to do something that involves working with my hands, but I'm not sure exactly what I'll end up doing.

    I don't think we'll ever grow up on the inside. No matter how old we get I think we'll always be two little girls who like getting dirty and playing dress up.
                                                                Breanne L.- age 11

Writing Sample

The following essay uses this pattern: comparing
comparing
contrasting

Nessie and Big Foot

They don't exist. Yet, they are famous. Footprints and farfetched sightings are all we have to go on and yet we choose to believe in them. They are the Loch Ness monster and Big Foot.

The stories of Big Foot and the Loch Ness monster, or Nessie, as she is called, are both shrouded by mystery. Neither creature has ever been proven or disproven to exist. The original stories date back to hundreds of years ago. "Sightings" have been reported for many years by many different people. People have even taken photos of these two monsters though most of them are considered to be a hoax. Though they are constantly searched for, it seems that only people who aren't looking for them ever claim to see these creatures.

Throughout all this time Nessie and Big Foot have become very well-known. When people found out how much other people were interested in these creatures, they started making things like Nessie stuffed animals and the monster truck, Big Foot. The Loch Ness monster and Big Foot are now household names and moneymakers.

Many other monsters like Big Foot have been reported in other parts of the world, whereas Nessie has only been spotted in Loch Ness, Scotland. Nessie is said to be some sort of water dinosaur, while Big Foot is believed to be a seven to ten foot tall ape man. More evidence exists to support Nessie than Big Foot, such as the fact that (if she exists) Nessie is officially protected wildlife.

Do they really exist? Are they out there? Some say there isn't enough evidence, while others believe in these supposedly nonexistent creatures. Will we ever know the truth, or will it forever remain an unsolved mystery?

Breanne L.- age 12

Writing Sample

The next essay uses this pattern: contrasting
                                    contrasting
                                    comparing

Red Sox and Yankees

The air is tense. It's hard to breathe. For a moment, all you can do is watch as the pitcher winds up and fires a strike. The rivalry as old as baseball itself has now begun once more. Welcome to opening day between the Boston Red Sox and the New York Yankees. Both teams are so different, yet so much alike. The intensity grows from minute to minute, from generation to generation.

If you look at the stats for each team over the years, you will notice a large difference that stands out. That difference is the number of World Series won. The Red Sox have won seven World Series, while the Yankees have won twenty-six. For many decades the Yankees set the standard for being an elite baseball team, but recently the tide seems to have turned. The Yankees have not won any recent World Series, while the Red Sox have won two in the past few years and now seem to be the dominant team.

The players are what affect the success of a team the most, and each team has had many great players. The Yankees had Babe Ruth, possibly the greatest player of all time. He began to thrive immediately after the Yankees acquired him early in his career. He went on to set many records and became a fan favorite. Years later, the Red Sox had a young star named Ted Williams. Ted was thought by many to be the greatest hitter ever. He might have broken many of Ruth's records if he hadn't served in World War II, taking time away from his baseball career. Both teams had many more unique players who contributed to their team's success.

Even though there is so much animosity between the Red Sox and Yankees, they are both a lot alike in many ways. Both teams are in the same division. During the season they play against some of the same opponents. Also, many players have played for both teams. Both the Yankees and Red Sox have left memories in the hearts of their fans, impressions that will last a lifetime.

The Red Sox and Yankees are two very talented baseball teams with extremely large numbers of dedicated fans. They play hard every game and are always fun to watch. Does history make one team better than the other? Does recent dominance outweigh the past? That is for you to decide.

David L.- age 15

Hands-On Activities

 Choose two things to compare and contrast. Sample topics can be found on page 72.

 Make a Venn diagram on paper or by using physical objects. For example, you can use two hula hoops and index cards to make a Venn diagram.

 Write a comparing/contrasting essay using one of the formats on page 37.

Lesson 11: Persuasive Essays

Goal: Write a persuasive essay.

 Watch the video lesson titled, *Persuasive Essays.*

Key Points

☞ A persuasive essay presents a point of view, and attempts to persuade the reader to agree.

☞ The thesis statement must be debatable. If it can't be opposed, you don't have a strong topic for a persuasive essay.

☞ Take a clear position on what you believe. A persuasive essay must never sound wishy-washy. If you don't choose one side of the argument and stick to it, you won't be able to persuade your reader.

☞ Use strong arguments, not assertions. An assertion makes a statement, but doesn't reason it out. An argument shows the reasoning, or evidence, behind what is said.

☞ Begin with your weakest argument to prove your point, and end with your strongest argument. If you're writing a timed essay, put your strongest argument first so you won't run out of time before you get to it.

You can use these persuasion techniques:
- State facts that can be proven.
- Use statistics.
- Offer quotes from experts.
- Use specific examples or stories, including personal examples from your own life.
- Give examples found in publications or in your school studies.

☞ Know your audience. Do they agree with you, disagree, or are they neutral about your subject? This will help you know which points to make and what evidence to provide to support your points.

☞ Put yourself in the shoes of someone who has the opposite point of view from yours. What arguments would this person have to disprove your points? Address their main arguments in your essay and prove why your point of view is more logical and believable. Be more convincing than your opponent.

The pen is mightier than the sword.
-Edward Bulwer-Lytton

Writing Sample

On the next few pages you will find two persuasive essays about the topic of issuing guns to teachers in schools. My essay offers one point of view and Susanna's essay shows the other side.

Guns Aren't the Answer

Pow! Pow! Pow! The unfamiliar sound of gunshots pierced the quiet Amish countryside as Charles Carl Roberts massacred innocent school girls in a one room schoolhouse. Unfortunately, this tragedy is only one of many similar school shootings that have occurred in the last decade. In an effort to combat this violence, some government officials are proposing that guns be issued to school teachers. I believe that putting guns in the hands of school teachers is dangerous, sets a bad example, and doesn't address the root problem, which is the moral decline of our society.

By issuing guns to teachers, we aren't decreasing the chance of school violence, but rather increasing the potential for harm. With more guns available, the chance increases that they will fall into the wrong hands. How will the guns be made readily accessible and yet kept safely out of reach of children? What are the chances that a teacher might be overpowered by a disgruntled student who could use the gun for harm? How do we know that we aren't handing a gun to a mentally unstable teacher? Additionally, teachers would require extensive training in the proper use of a firearm, which would mean more tax dollars when we barely have enough to go around right now. One of the biggest dangers is making the judgment call of when to use the gun. We would be asking teachers to make a split second decision that police officers with years of training have difficulty making.

If we put guns in the hands of teachers, how will that impact students? Teachers are role models, so it would appear that we're advocating violence if we hand them guns. Not only that, but we desensitize students to seeing violent weapons. Scientists say that when we see something over and over, it no longer produces a sense of shock. We simply become used to seeing it. This is the reason that T.V. shows are becoming increasingly immoral and violent, because people are so desensitized to immorality and violent acts that they seem like a part of normal life. Do we really want kids to become accustomed to seeing weapons in everyday life? What about the element of fear? Kids might be frightened by a teacher that resembles a prison guard. I don't think teachers with guns would have a positive impact on students.

Issuing guns to teachers is like putting a Band-Aid on someone who is hemorrhaging. It treats a small symptom while ignoring the bigger problem. The school shootings are simply a reflection of the moral and spiritual decline of our nation. We live in a society that doesn't value human life like it once did. Kids aren't taught that it's wrong to hurt another human. Instead, they grow up watching killing and violence on T.V. so it seems natural and normal to them. The boundary lines that once governed human behavior don't exist anymore. Morals have fallen by the wayside and people do what they want, not what is right. Until we bring morality back to our country, all the guns in the world won't help in the classroom.

Kids and guns don't mix. Any attempt to put the two together will result in more harm than good. Rather than treating symptoms, we need to get to the root issue and change the moral temperament of our society. Teachers don't need guns at their sides. Our society needs a change of heart and a return to old-fashioned morals and values.

B.L.

A Way to Save Lives

Whether or not teachers should have a gun in the classroom is a difficult decision to make, but I, for one, stand for it. Yes, maybe some teachers who shouldn't get a gun will get one, or a student will manage to get it away from a teacher, but if it's a possible way to stop needless deaths, we should use it. Hopefully, it will cause students to stop and think about the consequences of their actions. As the students won't have the superior fire power anymore, teachers will be better set up to protect their classrooms. It would also be kept a relative secret of who does have a gun, making it less likely for them to be stolen.

One thing that gives kids courage to bring in their own guns and shoot people is the knowledge that the teachers have limited ways of stopping them. They believe that they have the upper hand, the control. If there is the knowledge that a teacher might have a gun, they will be faced with the fact that they are no longer in control. Someone else will also have the power, and they won't know which teachers truly do have the power to fight back.

If they decide to issue guns to teachers, the teachers *will* have a better way of protecting their students and/or stopping the 'bad guys'. This would hopefully cut down on the death rate and offer a more effective way of maintaining control instead of just hoping for the best.

Finally, the program is supposed to be set up with a test and training for the teachers so that they won't be as much of a threat to the students. The tests should be set up to pick the teachers that are more stable, and not the ones that might become the 'bad guys'. Also, every teacher wouldn't have a gun and it wouldn't be announced which ones had them, making it very difficult to steal from a teacher.

Combined, I think this would be the most effective and safe way of protecting the schools and preventing more loss of life out of a lack of preparedness and lack of ability. Altogether, it's better to have more force on the good side, and save life, than it is to be worried about the dangers and lose lives.

Susanna S. - age 15

Hands-On Activities

 Look at Susanna's essay on page 47. Underline the thesis statement. Hint: You won't find it in the usual place. She has found a new spot within the first paragraph that works well for this particular paper.

 Choose a topic for a persuasive essay. Make sure you feel strongly about the topic. Sample topics can be found on page 73.

 Write a thesis statement. Then write a thesis statement from the opposing viewpoint. This will ensure that your thesis statement is debatable.

 Write a persuasive essay about the topic you've chosen.

Lesson 12: Revising the Essay

> Goal: Revise and polish an essay.

 Watch the video lesson titled, *Revising the Essay.*

Key Points

☞ Everything you write is a rough draft until it is revised and polished. All writing has room for improvement.

☞ Revision means to improve, not totally rewrite the essay.

☞ My #1 revision tip: Write something and put it aside for a few days. Then read it aloud, word by word, and you'll discover mistakes and areas needing improvement.

☞ Use a proofreading checklist to help revise your essay. See page 50 for an example. The same proofreading checklist appears on the last page of this book for easy reference.

☞ Critique unto others as you would have them critique unto you. Start with praise first, and then discuss areas needing improvement.

> *There is no great writing, only great rewriting.*
> *- Justice Brandeis*

Proofreading Checklist

- Is my essay written in standard essay format?
    - -Five paragraphs?
    - -Introduction?
    - -Three paragraphs in the body?
    - -Conclusion?

- Do I have a hook at the beginning?

- Do I have a clear thesis statement in the introduction?

- Does each middle paragraph have a topic sentence and supporting evidence?

- Does the conclusion wrap it up without giving new information about my topic?

- Have I written in complete sentences?

- Do all of my sentences begin with a capital letter and end with a punctuation mark?

- Did I indent paragraphs?

- Did I check the spelling of words I wasn't sure how to spell?

- Is my paper neat and easy to read?

- Did I do my best work?

Writing Sample

Breanne wrote a rough draft of an essay about softball. Compare her rough draft to the proofreading checklist and answer the questions. Read the polished copy of the essay and note changes made to the original paper.

Softball

Softball is a great sport for kids of all ages. It is a good team sport and teaches hand eye coordination and quick reflexes.

Softball is a good sport because it makes you get active and do exercise while you're having fun. In softball it is essential to have the right equipment. The basic stuff you need is a glove, a bat, cleats, and a helmet. Some people have extra safety equipment such as a mouth guard, batting gloves, shin guards, and sliding pads.

Softball is a good sport for people who like to think a lot during the game. To play softball you need at least nine players per team to play the nine positions which include catcher, pitcher, 1st, 2nd, and 3rd base, shortstop, and the three outfield positions.

I myself am a first baseman, but there are many other positions and I hope that you will try them someday.
                                                                    Breanne L.- age 11

Revised version:

Softball Stats

Kids play it. Dads play it. Moms play it. What is it? It's softball, of course. Softball is a great sport for kids of all ages.

Softball makes you get active and exercise while you're having fun at the same time. You have to keep your eye on the ball at the same time you're swinging the bat which teaches good hand eye coordination. You also need quick reflexes so you can catch balls that do unexpected things. Your arms get a workout from throwing and batting and if you hit well you'll be sprinting around the bases.

In softball, it's essential to have the right equipment. The basic stuff you need is a glove, a bat, cleats, and a helmet. Some people have extra safety equipment such as mouth guards, batting gloves, shin guards, and sliding pads.

Softball is a sport for people who enjoy thinking and teamwork. To play softball you need nine players to cover all the positions which include catcher, pitcher, first, second and third bases, shortstop and three outfield positions. When you catch the ball you have to think about where to throw it next. You need to watch what your teammates are doing and keep an eye on the batter and runners from the opposing team. Everyone on the team has to stay alert, think about what's happening, and work together.

Softball is fun for everyone. If you've never played before, you should try it. Only watch out because I'm the first baseman and I'm going to get you out!

Breanne L.- age 11

Hands-On Activities

 Choose an essay that you've already written for this course, one that you would like to revise.

 Use the proofreading checklist to help make revisions to your essay.

 If you have someone who can read your paper and offer suggestions, this would be a good time to get help.

 As neatly as possible, write or type the polished paper.

Lesson 13: Developing Your Writing Style

Goal: Develop your own unique style of writing.

 Watch the video lesson titled,
Developing Your Writing Style.

Key Points

 Style is like your fingerprints.
It's a way of writing that is uniquely your own.

 In writing essays, you are free to express your own style.

 Some things should be a part of every writer's style, just as in the video each of the fashion models wore his or her own style of clothing.

 This is a list of elements of style that should be included in everyone's writing:
- Show, don't tell (covered in Lesson 9)
- Active writing instead of passive writing (page 57)
- Writing tight (page 58)
- Smooth flow (page 59-60)

Every artist was first an amateur.
-Ralph Waldo Emerson

Writing Sample

Read the following writing samples from different writers. Each one has an individual style and sound to it. Try to visualize the writer as you read each piece.

Dear Aunt Stephanie,

    Thank you very much for the $100. I went to the mall and went crazy. It was so much fun. I still haven't spent it all yet, but trust me, I will. Maybe we could go shopping together with some of it. I will save the rest for my expensive drama class. You are such a wonderful aunt and I am glad I have you!

    Love,
    Heather

Heather T.- age 14

    Well, here I am on earth. It's very green and there are all sorts of strange life forms that are obsessed with fashion and driven by the media. The climate varies, either it's cloudy, rainy, or sunny. The length of time here is sixty seconds to a minute, sixty minutes to an hour, 24 hours to a day, 7 days to a week, 4 weeks to a month, and 12 months to a year. An unusual fact is gravity which holds you down. Cool, huh?

Stewart M.- age 12

    If you saw me, you'd probably say in your head, "This guy is crazy and scary and kind of smells." All that might be true, but it's because of my upbringing a.k.a. my parents and brother. The reason I'm kind of crazy is because of all the things that have happened in the past that might have knocked off more than a few brain cells. For example, one time my brother and I were in the back yard and we were bored so we decided to hit golf balls in the air with a tennis racket. As you can see, this is not a good combination. My brother hit a golf ball as high as he could, but as it was coming down the sun got in my eyes and the next thing I felt was something smash into my skull. The golf ball hit me so hard that I fell backward and started crying.

Austin W.- age 16

Writing Sample

"Me and Her"

I'm loud, she's quiet. I'm sad, she's happy. I'm disobedient; she's sitting on her hands. We've laughed together, cried together, and snuck out of the house at one in the morning together. Who is this person that is both the opposite and exact same as me? Her name is Allison and she is my best friend. We're not totally different, but I can't say we're exactly the same. That may be what makes us such good friends.

She's crazy- I'm crazier. She's loud- I can be louder. She's smart- okay never mind. She likes swimming and I like soccer. We are the same completely, and at the same time 100% different.

It's easy to see that these are the reasons we are such good friends. We both love junk food. And when it comes to keeping secrets- I know that she's the woman to go to.

We grew up together and haven't always been tight, but I do know one thing. No matter what, this friendship will never die.

Yep, I've got to put up with her for a lifetime!

Laura A.- age 13

The Pearl Locket

I was strolling the baby up the smooth black road glancing at people's verdant lawns when I noticed my friend, Bill, was having a yard sale. He had tools, clothes, toys, and jewelry. Since Mother's Day was soon, I bought a special locket for Mom.

At home I cleaned the locket and opened it. To my horror there was a picture of my mom and Stalin! I couldn't believe it. As much as I hated prying, I had to do it for my country. I started in Mom's office and ended in her closet. Nothing.

In the attic I did find a few things- red paper, a brick red wig, and a crimson cape. I didn't find any Russian texts or weapons.

Next I checked her computer to see if the password was Russia. I also checked the computer's screen saver to make sure it wasn't a picture of Moscow.

I decided to confront Mom. I made a surprise entrance through the laundry chute and confronted her. "That's your Uncle Mort," she said. "He owns a bagel shop in Manhattan." What a relief! She saved me a trip to the FBI.

Johnnie C.- age 14

Hands-On Activities

 Look over the essays you've written so far. Do you notice a certain style or personality in your writing?

 The exercises included with this lesson will help you develop the essential elements of style necessary for well-written essays. Complete the *Active Versus Passive Writing* exercise on page 57.

 Complete the *Writing Tight* exercise on page 58.

 Complete the *Go with the Flow* exercise on page 59.

 Complete the *Use Transition Words* exercise on page 60.

Essential Elements of Style

The following exercises will help you learn some things about style that every writer should know.

Active Versus Passive Writing:

In active writing, the subject of a simple sentence is the one taking action and is found at the beginning of the sentence. The receiver of the action is later in the sentence, after the action has taken place. An active sentence is strong, and is the proper way to organize a sentence. It looks like this:

<u>subject</u> – <u>action</u> - <u>receiver of the action</u>.

Active Voice Example: Jimmy – throws - the ball.

In passive writing, the receiver of the action is placed in the subject position at the beginning of a simple sentence. The subject, the one taking action, is no longer at the beginning of the sentence. A passive sentence is weak, and it is not the proper way to organize a sentence. It looks like this:

<u>receiver of the action</u> – <u>action</u> - <u>subject</u>.

Passive Voice Example: The ball   - is thrown -   by Jimmy.

In most cases, active voice makes your writing lively and more interesting than passive voice.

Convert the following sentences from passive to active voice. I have done an example for you.

Passive: The big fat rat was caught by my sweet little kitty.
Active: My sweet little kitty caught the big fat rat.

1. Grandma received a speeding ticket from the police officer.

2. All of the jelly beans were eaten by the writing class.

3. A huge cell phone bill was created by Molly.

4. Feathery soft whiskers were shaved off by Jeff.

5. An entire large pizza was polished off by two teenage girls.

Writing Tight:

Don't let your words run loose and wild. Say what you mean in the most effective manner possible. Keep it short. Keep it simple. Keep it right on target.

Read this example of a loose sentence that has been tightened:

Loose:
She had blonde hair and had something to say about everything.

Tight:
She was a mouthy blonde.

Tighten the following loose sentences:
1. Those who drive while under the influence of alcohol might get a night in jail or hurt or kill someone.

2. It seems to me that more and more violence is becoming acceptable on T.V. shows.

3. You know, I just think like that all girls should like you know dress modestly and all.

4. Hard as it might be to believe or to understand or to comprehend, I can actually write a full-fledged essay now.

Go With the Flow:

Writing can feel like riding down a bumpy gravel road, or it can be as smooth as a ride in a luxury limousine. Ideally, you want the writing to flow as smoothly as possible. These tips will help improve the flow.

Combine sentences

Choppy writing: Todd is a boy. He is skinny. He is young.
Smooth flow: Todd is a skinny, young boy.

It's your turn.
Choppy writing: Spaghetti is a dog. He is a male. He is big.
Smooth flow:

Shorten rambling sentences

Rambling sentence: We drove forever and I thought we'd never get there, but we finally did and was it ever worth the wait because I got to ride the fastest rollercoaster around and it was so much fun I could have ridden it forever.

Smooth flow: We drove forever and I thought we'd never get there. It was worth the wait because I got to ride the fastest rollercoaster around. It was so much fun, and I could have ridden it forever.

It's your turn again.
Rambling sentence: I went to my friend's house and we played games and we ate pizza and we rode bikes and ate some more pizza and then we went to sleep and woke up and watched T.V. and had more pizza for breakfast.

Smooth flow:

Use Transition Words:

Transition words are words that connect thoughts so that the writing doesn't abruptly start and stop.

Example: I worked hard on my writing assignments. <u>Finally</u>, I reached lesson 16 in my writing curriculum and completed the course.

This is a list of transition words and phrases you can use in your writing to create a smooth flow. Many more words can be added. As you think of them add them to the bottom of the list.

finally	*in conclusion*	*next*
evidently	*however*	*then*
in addition	*yet*	*indeed*
therefore	*for example*	*perhaps*
for instance	*first*	*in fact*

Lesson 14: Understanding Prompts

Goal: Understand prompts and take appropriate action.

 Watch the video lesson titled, *Understanding Prompts*.

Key Points

 A prompt gives instructions about what you are to write. It may include a quote, information, and instructions.

 Read the prompt very carefully.

 Look for question marks.

 Underline command words. Command words are the words that tell you what action to take. For example, as you read through the key points on this page you will see the following command words: read, look, underline, and follow.

 Follow the instructions given in the prompt when writing your essay.

Sit down to write what you have thought, and not to think about what you shall write.
-William Cobbett

Writing Sample

Read the prompts below.

We want no war of conquest. War should never be entered upon until every agency of peace has failed.
                            President William McKinley

War is a highly controversial subject. Consider the quote. Do you believe war should always be a last resort after every attempt at peace is exhausted? Decide your point of view and write an essay that explains your reasoning.

Most folks are about as happy as they make up their minds to be.
                            President Abraham Lincoln

So many people seek happiness. Some find it, others don't. Is happiness purely a decision of the mind? Write an essay that explains your point of view.

Nearly all men can stand adversity, but if you want to test a man's character, give him power.
                            President Abraham Lincoln

Think about this quote. Do you believe that putting a person in a position of power will reveal his true nature, whether good or bad? Plan and write an essay that illustrates your point of view.

Restlessness is discontent- and discontent is the first necessity of progress. Show me a thoroughly satisfied man- and I will show you a failure.

Thomas Edison

Like Thomas Edison, some people believe that discontentment and past failures spur people to make progress in life. What do you think? Are discontentment and past failures the secret to success? Write an essay explaining your position.

State a moral case to a plowman and a professor. The former will decide it well, often better than the latter, because he has not been led astray by artificial rules.

President Thomas Jefferson

To educate, or not to educate, that is the question. Many in our society feel that formal education is essential to make one wise. Thomas Jefferson had a different opinion. What do you think? Is formal education which extends beyond high school overrated? Write an essay expressing your opinion.

The notion of political correctness has ignited controversy across the land. And although the movement arises from the laudable desire to sweep away the debris of racism and sexism and hatred, it replaces old prejudices with new ones.

It declares certain topics to be off-limits, certain expressions to be off-limits, even certain gestures to be off-limits. What began as a crusade for civility has soured into a cause of conflict and even censorship.

President George Bush

What do you think? Is the idea of political correctness just another form of prejudice or is it essential to a civilized society? Organize your thoughts and write a persuasive essay that explains your point of view.

Hands-On Activities

 Several prompts are listed on pages 62-63. The student should circle the question marks in the prompts and underline the command words. Command words are the words that tell what action should be taken.

 Choose a prompt from pages 62-63 that you will use to write an essay in the next lesson.

Lesson 15: Timed Writing

> Goal: Write an essay in 25 minutes.

 Watch the video lesson titled, *Timed Writing*.

Key Points

 When you are facing a timed writing, remain calm and focused.

 Have a plan of action.

 This is a reasonable plan of action for a 25 minute time limit:
1. Read and understand the prompt. (1 minute)
2. Develop your point of view and thesis statement. (1 minute)
3. Brainstorm your thoughts and create a short outline. (2-3 minutes)
4. Write the essay. (17-18 minutes)
5. Use any leftover time to proofread and revise.

 Don't waste time dawdling or daydreaming. If you finish early, use the remainder of the time to read and improve your essay.

There is no perfect time to write, there is only now.
-Barbara Kingsolver

Writing Sample

This essay uses one of the prompts listed on page 63. It's an example of an essay written in 25 minutes.

Restlessness is discontent- and discontent is the first necessity of progress. Show me a thoroughly satisfied man- and I will show you a failure.

Thomas Edison

Like Thomas Edison, some people believe that discontentment and past failures spur people to make progress in life. What do you think? Are discontentment and past failures the secret to success? Write an essay explaining your position.

Losing to Win?

Can losers be winners? History is full of stories of people who went through great losses before meeting success. Some folks even believe that suffering loss or feeling discontent is the secret ingredient of success. I disagree. While some people use failure to propel them forward, countless others are completely devastated by it. The key to success isn't how much we fail or how discontent we feel, but success comes to those who are motivated, hard working, and persistent.

Successful people are motivated people. They don't wait around for someone to tell them what to do. Instead, they find a cause or idea and run with it. The Wright brothers come to mind. They had the notion that man can fly. They believed it with their whole hearts, and this belief motivated them to spend months at a time, and most of their money, camped out at Kitty Hawk trying to create a flying machine. Like the Wright brothers, successful people find the fuel within themselves to keep them moving forward.

Hard workers also meet success in life. For example, my parents are two of the hardest workers I've ever known. Both of them hold down full time jobs and work overtime. In addition, they devote time to raising money for charity.

When they're at home you'll find them busy with housekeeping and yard work. As a result, they enjoy many of the benefits of success, such as a lovely home, a measure of financial freedom, and the satisfaction of a job well done.

The greatest key to success is persistence. It's the "never give up" attitude. Colonel Sanders is a prime example. He experimented with chicken recipes for years before discovering the Kentucky Fried Chicken recipe at the age of sixty-five. Jan Karon is another example. She left a lucrative job to follow a dream. She spent two penniless years writing, only to have her book rejected multiple times before it was finally published as the first in the Mitford series. Today we know her as a bestselling author, but years of persistence brought her to this place.

Yes, losers can be winners, but experiencing failure and discontentment isn't a guarantee of success. Only those who are motivated, willing to work hard, and refuse to give up will succeed in reaching their dreams. As the old saying goes, "It's not whether you win or lose, but how you play the game." Regardless of past failures or successes, those who play by the right set of rules will enjoy a measure of success.
B.L.

Hands-On Activities

 Choose a prompt from pages 62-63.

 Using the prompt you chose, write an essay in 25 minutes. Do your best, but don't be discouraged if you don't complete the essay within the time limit. This is precisely why you need to practice writing essays over and over, so that you can write within a specific time frame. This will come in handy in your schoolwork, in college, and on standardized tests such as the SAT.

Lesson 16: The Wrap Up

Goal: Continue writing essays until it becomes easy for you.

 Watch the video lesson titled, *The Wrap Up.*

Key Points

☞ Continue watching the videos and using this program until you master the essay.

☞ Write a lot of essays. You learn to write by practicing.

☞ Remember: If you have a brain and you have a hand, you can write an essay!

| *By writing much one learns to write well.* |
| *-Isaac Bashevis Singer* |

Writing Sample

You've read many examples throughout this program. Now, it's your turn! You're ready, qualified, and able to write an excellent essay. Turn to the *Writing Ideas* section on pages 70-74, and choose the type of essay you'd like to write.

Celebrate your Accomplishment!

Now is the time to use those persuasive writing skills you have learned. Brainstorm ways you might like to celebrate your accomplishment. Choose one idea, and write an essay persuading your parents to reward you for a job well done!

Writing Ideas

Expository Essay Topics and Examples

Write an essay explaining how to do something.
- How to pretend you're doing schoolwork when you're really not
- How to really get on your mom's nerves in three easy steps
- How to gross everyone out at the supper table

Give an explanation of your favorite game or sport.
- Drag racing for beginners
- The hidden strategies behind *Chutes and Ladders*™
- The basics of watermelon seed spitting

Provide information on a topic you know well.
- Ways to make money without officially getting a job
- The annoying habits of the common house fly
- Rare diseases of life forms on other planets

Explain why you like something.
- The top three reasons why you love the stuffed monkey you've had since you were a baby
- Why you absolutely adore writing essays
- The best traits of that good-looking human who looks back at you in the mirror each day

Offer clarification on an issue
- Why you can never keep your room clean
- What your sister really wants when she offers to do chores
- How you managed to drive the car through the garage door

Descriptive Essay Topics and Examples

Your dream house
- A rambling mansion in Beverly Hills
- A tent pitched on Mt. Everest
- The sidecar on your Harley Davidson

Your dream car
- An original Model T
- A high-powered sports car
- One that runs

Your dream wedding
- A posh million dollar event on a tropical island
- A quiet romantic exchanging of vows with just family present
- One where you bolt for the door before you say, "I do."

Your favorite place
- A dry towel spread out on the beach
- The all-you-can-eat buffet at the local greasy spoon
- Anywhere your brother or sister is not

A person who interests you
- Mrs. Lillie on the videos
- The old lady on the videos
- Your grandma's uncle's cousin's nephew's neighbor's son's barber

Comparing/Contrasting Essay Topics and Examples

Two restaurants –
- The Greasy Chicken / Bubba's Big Boy BBQ

Two lifestyles
-The life of a health nut / that of a junk food junkie

Two animals
- Your neighbor's pet / your dog who ate the neighbor's pet

Two wars
-The Revolutionary War / Star Wars

Two jobs or careers
-The job of a homeschooling parent / the job of a rocket scientist

Two types of writing
- An essay / a police report

Two foods
- A triple-decker, loaded-to-the gills hamburger / tofu

Two cultures of people
- A teenager / a politician

Two places
- Here /somewhere else

Two people
- The old lady on the video / Mrs. Lillie, the teacher on the video

Persuasive Essay Topics and Examples

Your soapbox issue
- Kids should be allowed to keep their rooms as messy as they want.
- Writing essays is hazardous to your health.

Something you'd like to change
- The way your mother drives
- Your Uncle Smitty's grooming habits

Persuading your parents
- To let you sell your brother or sister
- That schoolwork is totally unnecessary in the grand scheme of things

A controversial issue
- Can groundhogs see shadows?
- Is there really a pot of gold at the end of the rainbow?

A political issue
- Management of illegal aliens from other planets
- Lowering the voting age to 5

Something that angers you
- The plight of fleas at pet grooming salons
- Having to eat your vegetables

A worthy cause
- A campaign to open a Unicorn Research Institute
- Generating money to support the Overworked, Underpaid Teenager Fund of America

Narrative Essay Topics and Examples

Remember that a narrative essay narrates or tells a story. Think *Goldilocks*.

A family story
- The tale of Grandma getting run over by the reindeer

A happy day
- The day your parents finally got caught up on your allowance

A sad event
- The time great Aunt Tessie accidentally sat on your gerbil--God rest his soul.

An embarrassing time
- When your parents proudly showed your naked baby pictures at your birthday party

A proud moment
- The first time you downed an entire extra large pizza by yourself

A moment to remember
- How National Static Electricity Day came to be

A funny happening
- When your dad dressed up as an old lady for your mother's writing videos

Resources for Researching Topics

If you need to research your topic, you might want to use some of the resources listed below. Please get your parent's permission before using the Internet.

- www.encyclopedia.com - This is an online encyclopedia. You can also use a hardback encyclopedia that you might have at home or find in your local library, but make sure you are using a current issue and not an outdated book.

- You can also use Internet search engines such as www.google.com, www.bing.com, or www.ask.com. Simply go to the site and type in the name of your topic, and you will be provided with other websites which contain the information that you need.

- Don't forget about your local library. Books and magazines can be helpful sources of information. If you can't find what you need, the librarian can assist you in your search.

- Depending on your topic, it may help to interview someone who knows a lot about the subject. For example, if you want to learn about pottery, you might find a local potter whom you can consult. Don't be shy with your questions. Generally, people like to talk about what they do.

- Field trips may be a helpful way to learn about your topic, as well. For example, you might visit a local museum or historical site. Touring factories or businesses may also be helpful. Paying a visit to a college or specialty school may give you a chance to learn more about your subject.

How to Evaluate Writing
(a section for parents and evaluators)

> The first goal of writing is to build confidence in the writer.

A student who believes he can write will write. It's much more difficult to teach a student who doesn't believe that he can write.

> Praise goes a long ways.

Memorize the rhyme above and make it your motto when evaluating writing.

Approach every paper looking for what is right and good, not for what is wrong.

Always start by listing the strengths of the writing. List them all, every single one that you can find. Find one or two areas that need improvement, and help the writer find ways to remedy those issues.

> Focus on content.

Look for imagination, style, choice of topic, sensory details, supporting evidence--the pillars of great writing!

Lesson by Lesson Evaluations

In this section, I will take you lesson by lesson and tell you exactly what to look for as you evaluate your student's work.

Lesson 1: *Hands-On Essay* Demonstration

The student will be able to demonstrate to you the *Hands-On Essay* format using his own hand, without consulting the book or the videos.

Page 3 lists the parts of the *Hands-On Essay* format, and you can follow along as the student demonstrates for you.

Lesson 2: Know Your Audience

In this lesson, the student will identify the audience for the expository essay, which will be written over the next few lessons. Discuss the written answers to the following questions:
1. Who is my audience?
2. What do they expect from me?

FYI, an expository essay explains, instructs, informs, or clarifies.

Lesson 3: Choosing a Topic

In this session, the student will choose a topic and brainstorm that topic. I recommend that the first time around you get involved in the process by discussing the questions listed on page 10. Once the topic has been decided, help the student brainstorm the subject using an idea web like the one on page 9.

Lesson 4: Outlining the Essay

Once again, you may need to assist your student in creating an outline like the one on page 13. It may be difficult for your student to complete the outline the first time through this course. It's okay if it is completed over the next several lessons as the student learns the *Hands-On Essay* format in more depth. The process should be easier after the completion of the first essay.

Lesson 5: Hooking the Reader

Read the hook the student has written for the expository essay. The hook is the opening part of the essay that grabs the reader's attention and makes him want to read more. For examples of hooks, read pages 17-19.

The whole idea is to be different, not boring. You want the reader to give the essay a thumbs up from the very beginning.

Lesson 6: Creating a Thesis Statement

The thesis statement is the one sentence that tells the topic of the essay. For more information read pages 21-23.

Ideally, the student will write the thesis statement for the expository essay on a piece of paper, and show it to you or someone who does not know the topic of the essay. If the person can decipher the topic of the essay from the thesis statement alone, it's well written. If not, the student needs to try again.

In this lesson, the student will also use the hook and thesis statement to create the introductory paragraph of the expository essay. The paragraph should go from general information to a specific thesis statement. Think of a funnel shape that starts out wide and gradually narrows down.

Look for these three things:
-a hook that grabs the reader's attention
-a paragraph that goes from general to specific
-a thesis statement that clearly states the topic of the essay

Lesson 7: Developing the Body of the Essay

The student will write the three middle paragraphs, or the body, of the essay. For more information and samples, see pages 24-27.

As you evaluate these paragraphs, remember to focus on content. You will also look for a topic sentence in each paragraph that tells the subject of the paragraph. In addition, you'll look for details or supporting evidence to prove the point made in each paragraph. If your student has difficulty, you might first work through gathering evidence orally before writing the paragraphs.

Lesson 8: Writing the Conclusion

The conclusion summarizes the essay. One way to do this is by rewording the thesis statement in a new way. No new information about the topic appears in the concluding paragraph. The ending should leave the reader with something to think about, similar to the hook in the first paragraph. Look for these aspects in your student's conclusion.

The student should now combine all of the individual parts of the essay, and type it or write it neatly.

Lesson 9: Descriptive Essays

This time, the student will work through the *Hands-On Essay* process to write an essay that describes something, someone, or someplace. Once again, focus on content. Specifically look for vivid details that appeal to the senses.

Also, look for all of the components of an essay listed below:
- Introductory paragraph
- Hook
- Thesis statement
- Three middle paragraphs
- A topic sentence for each middle paragraph
- Details and supporting evidence in middle paragraphs
- A conclusion that summarizes, and leaves the reader thinking

 These are suggested revisions of the sentences on page 35. Individual responses will vary.

1. Ginger is a talented singer.　　　　Ginger is a skilled singer.

2. Paris is a breath-taking place!　　Paris is an artistic place!

3. He had a difficult day.　　　　　　He had a painful day.

4. I just read a thrilling story.　　　　I just read a memorable story.

5. The weather is sunny today.　　　The weather is fair today.

6. My friend drives an expensive car.　My friend drives a posh car.

Lesson 10: Comparing/Contrasting Essays

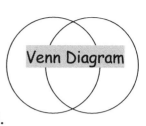

This assignment is an essay that compares and contrasts two things. To compare is to show similarities, and to contrast is to point out differences. The student should follow all the steps of the *Hands-On Essay* process.

Prior to writing the comparing/contrasting essay, the student should create a Venn diagram. See page 38 for an example. If the student is having trouble, you might ask questions that will assist the thinking process.

When evaluating the comparing/contrasting essay, pay special attention to how smoothly it flows. Ideas for organizing the paragraphs are given on pages 39-42. The essay should have some sort of pattern for pointing out similarities and differences, and not just contain random thoughts.

Lesson 11: Persuasive Essays

Once again, the student will follow all of the steps of the *Hands-On Essay* process to write a persuasive essay. As you evaluate it, focus on content. The essay should contain all of the parts of an essay listed on page 3.

The thesis statement is extremely important in a persuasive essay. It must clearly state the writer's point of view on the topic, no wishy-washy thinking allowed. It should be debatable. A persuasive essay topic must have an opposing viewpoint, or it's not a good topic.

The body of the essay should include strong arguments and convincing evidence. Think of an attorney trying to prove his case. It's also wise if the essay addresses a few of the opposing arguments, proving them to be wrong, or at least not as good as the writer's arguments. Read the essays on pages 45-47 to get the idea.

In the essay on page 47, Susanna put the thesis statement at the beginning of the introduction instead of its usual spot at the end of the first paragraph. Her thesis statement is this sentence: *Whether or not teachers should have a gun in the classroom is a difficult decision to make, but I, for one, stand for it.*

Lesson 12: Revising Your Essay

For this lesson, I can almost guarantee that you'll need to help the student the first time around. That does not mean that *you* should do the work. You are only the assistant on the project.

The assignment is to choose an essay from a former lesson and revise it. Walk with the student through the proofreading checklist found on pages 50 and 88. From now on, this checklist will be used by the student to proofread every essay written. A sample revision is found on pages 51-52.

Lesson 13: Developing Your Writing Style

I recommend that you read the lesson and the samples found on pages 54-56. The student will complete exercises on page 57-60. When they are completed, review them together.

 These are suggested revisions of the sentences found on pages 57-60. Individual responses will vary.

Page 57:
1. The police officer gave Grandma a speeding ticket.
2. The writing class ate all the jelly beans.
3. Molly created a huge cell phone bill.
4. Jeff shaved off his feathery, soft whiskers.
5. Two teenage girls polished off an entire large pizza.

Page 58:
1. Drunk drivers may end up in jail, hurt someone, or even kill someone.
2. I've noticed that violence is becoming more acceptable on T.V. shows.
3. I think all girls should dress modestly.
4. Believe it or not, I can write an essay now.

Page 59:
Spaghetti is a big, male dog.

I went to my friend's house. We played games, ate pizza, rode bikes, ate more pizza, and went to sleep. When we woke up we watched T.V. and had more pizza for breakfast.

Lesson 14: Understanding Prompts

Several writing prompts are listed on pages 62-63. The student should circle the question marks in the prompts and underline the command words. The point of the lesson is to learn how to read a prompt, understand it, and know what you're being asked to do. You might try discussing one or two of the prompts together to make sure the student understands them.

The student will also choose one prompt to use in the next lesson.

Command words found on page 62-63:

Prompt #1: consider, decide, write   Prompt #4: write

Prompt #2: write   Prompt #5: write

Prompt #3: think, plan, write   Prompt #6: organize, write

Lesson 15: Timed Writing

In this lesson, the student will use one of the prompts from pages 62-63 and write an essay in 25 minutes. A plan of action can be found on page 65.

When the essay is complete, you should look for all of the essay components:
- Introductory paragraph
- Hook
- Thesis statement
- Three middle paragraphs
- A topic sentence for each middle paragraph
- Details and supporting evidence in middle paragraphs
- A conclusion that summarizes, and leaves the reader thinking

Word to the wise: Your student may not complete an essay within 25 minutes the first few times. This is why it's so important to continue practicing writing essays, and writing timed essays, even when the student has completed this course.

Lesson 16: The Wrap Up

I strongly suggest that the student go through this course as many times as needed to absorb the information. Students learn to write by writing and writing and writing. However, your student just finished a challenging course. It's time to celebrate! Plan a way to reward your student for a job well done. CONGRATULATIONS!

Suggested Essay Assignments

Expository Essays

- Assign an essay that corresponds with what the student is studying in another subject. For example, if your student is studying oceanography, you might ask for an expository essay about a sea creature or ocean currents.

- Have your student write an essay about a special hobby or interest. It's more enjoyable to write about things you like or know well.

- If your student plays a sport, have him write an essay explaining how the sport is played.

- Perhaps you and your student are experiencing a communication gap. Assign an essay that gives your student a chance to explain something she feels you don't understand. For example, if you don't see eye to eye on clothing styles, assign an essay that gives her a chance to explain current fashions.

Descriptive Essays

- Most kids treasure the idea of designing and decorating their own rooms. Ask your student to write an essay describing his or her dream room if the budget was unlimited.

- Have your student write about his hero. Remind him to include more than just physical traits in his description. He should include the characteristics that make this person his hero.

- Assign an essay in which the student describes himself. This paper should include more than just facts. It should include how he perceives himself. Does he see himself as someone who is witty, handsome, creative, or intelligent? Be sure he includes examples to prove the point.

- Ask the student to describe his favorite place. This can be anything from a booming metropolitan city to a very common, simple place. For example, my cousin is a musician who once wrote an essay about his piano bench, which is his favorite place in the world.

Comparing/Contrasting Essays

- Have your student compare and contrast two careers that he might be interested in for the future.

- Ask your student to compare and contrast two time periods. For example, he might compare and contrast the life of teenagers in the present with the life of teenagers in Colonial times.

- If you have upcoming elections in your area, have your student compare and contrast the candidates.

- Ask your student to write an essay comparing and contrasting what he was like as a young child, with what he is like at present.

Persuasive Essays

- If your student is trying to convince you of something, turn that persuasive power into an essay. For example, if your student wants to attend a particular college, he can write an essay outlining why he thinks that college would be best.

- Does your student have strong feelings about a particular issue? Maybe he feels strongly about capital punishment or child abuse. Turn that emotion into a persuasive essay where he tries to convince others to see his point of view.

- Pretend that your student is running for political office. Have him write a persuasive essay as his campaign speech.

- Watch the news or look through the newspaper and assign a persuasive essay based on a current event. Make sure the student does a little research and takes a stand on one side of the issue.

Narrative Essays

- Ask your student to write a favorite family story in essay form.

- Have your student rewrite a famous day in history in his own words. Ideally, you want to choose a day which corresponds with his current history studies.

- Ask your student to pretend that he is someone else, a famous person, a friend, even a cartoon character, and write about his life.

- Have your student write an essay with any of the following titles:
  My Best Day Ever   *My Happiest Moment*
  The Saddest Time in My Life   *My Most Embarrassing Moment*
  A Time to Remember   *My Greatest Achievement*
  The Funniest Thing That Ever Happened to Me

Proofreading Checklist

- Is my essay written in standard essay format?
    - -Five paragraphs?
    - -Introduction?
    - -Three paragraphs in the body?
    - -Conclusion?

- Do I have a hook at the beginning?

- Do I have a clear thesis statement in the introduction?

- Does each middle paragraph have a topic sentence and supporting evidence?

- Does the conclusion wrap it up without giving new information about my topic?

- Have I written in complete sentences?

- Do all of my sentences begin with a capital letter and end with a punctuation mark?

- Did I indent paragraphs?

- Did I check the spelling of words I wasn't sure how to spell?

- Is my paper neat and easy to read?

- Did I do my best work?

Be sure to visit www.handsonessays.com and sign up for my free newsletter to receive even more writing tips and notice of the latest publications by Bonita Lillie Publishing!

Made in the USA
Lexington, KY
28 August 2015